MATH ACADEMY

SOLD ON SUBTRACTION

By Kirsty Holmes

CRABTREE
PUBLISHING COMPANY
WWW.CRABTREEBOOKS.COM

CRABTREE
PUBLISHING COMPANY
WWW.CRABTREEBOOKS.COM

Author:
Kirsty Holmes
Editorial director:
Kathy Middleton
Editors:
William Anthony, Janine Deschenes
Proofreader:
Crystal Sikkens
Graphic design:
Ian McMullen
Prepress technician:
Katherine Berti
Print coordinator:
Katherine Berti

All images are courtesy of Shutterstock.com, unless otherwise specified.
With thanks to Getty Images, Thinkstock Photo, and iStockphoto.

Front Cover: New Africa, ShutterStockStudio iunewind, vipman, Nadya_Art

Interior: Background – ngaga. Characters: Maya: Rajesh Narayanan. Zoe: Dave Pot. Robert: Shift Drive. Abdul: Ahmad Ihsan. Professor Tengent: Roman Samborskyi. Cy-Bud: AlesiaKan. 6–7 – Hortimages, Ilyashenko Oleksiy, Hulinska Yevheniia. 8 – grafvision, Aluna1. 10 – Africa Studio, vitalka_ka. 16 – Sweet Art, Katerina Sanna. 21 – Jeanette Dietl. 21– maramorosz

All facts, statistics, web addresses, and URLs in this book were verified as valid and accurate at time of writing. No responsibility for any changes to external websites or references can be accepted by either the author or publisher.

Library and Archives Canada Cataloguing in Publication

Title: Sold on subtraction / by Kirsty Holmes.
Names: Holmes, Kirsty, author.
Description: Series statement: Math academy | Includes index.
Identifiers: Canadiana (print) 20200394185 |
  Canadiana (ebook) 20200394207 |
  ISBN 9781427130129 (hardcover) |
  ISBN 9781427130167 (softcover) |
  ISBN 9781427130204 (HTML)
Subjects: LCSH: Subtraction—Juvenile literature.
Classification: LCC QA115 .H65 2021 | DDC j513.2/12—dc23

Library of Congress Cataloging-in-Publication Data

Available at the Library of Congress

Crabtree Publishing Company

www.crabtreebooks.com   1–800–387–7650
Published by Crabtree Publishing Company in 2021
© 2020 BookLife Publishing Ltd.

All rights reserved. No part of this publication may be reproduced, stored in a retrieval system or be transmitted in any form or by any means, electronic, mechanical, photocopying, recording, or otherwise, without the prior written permission of Crabtree Publishing Company.

Printed in the U.S.A./022021/CG20201123

Published in Canada
Crabtree Publishing
616 Welland Ave.
St. Catharines, Ontario
L2M 5V6

Published in the United States
Crabtree Publishing
347 Fifth Ave
Suite 1402-145
New York, NY 10016

CONTENTS

Words that are bold, like **this**, can be found in the glossary on page 24.

ATTENDANCE

Another day at Math Academy has begun. Time to take attendance! Meet some students in class 301.

Maya
Favorite subject:
Place value

Zoë
Favorite subject:
Counting in groups

Professor Tangent

Ali
Favorite subject:
Addition

Robert
Favorite subject:
Subtraction

Today's lesson is all about **subtraction**. The students will learn answers to these questions.

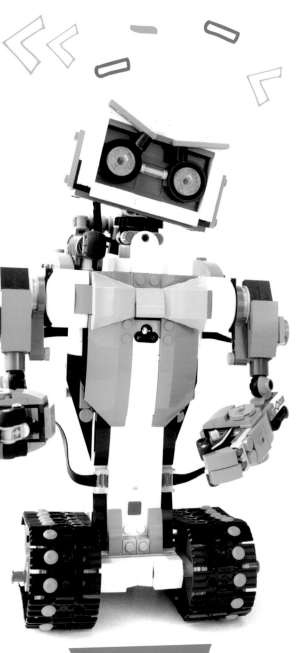

- What is subtraction?
- What is **place value**?
- How can I use **charts** and **number lines** to help me subtract?

Math Academy is a school especially for kids who love math and solving problems.

Do I hear the bell?

Cy-Bud

Favorite subject:
Facts and figures

MORNING LESSON

Class 301 is holding a sale in the playground. The students want to raise money to buy a new super-**calculator** for the classroom. Robert is going from table to table to write down how many items have been sold.

Let's start at Zoë's table. She is selling delicious lemonade.

At the start of the day, Zoë had nine jugs of lemonade. She has two jugs of lemonade left on the table. Robert and Zoë use subtraction to find how many jugs were sold. Subtraction is taking one number away from another to find a new number.

—

The minus sign is the **symbol** for subtraction.

=

The equals sign is the symbol that shows the number that is left after subtracting.

$$9 - 2 = 7$$

Zoë has sold seven jugs of lemonade.

LUNCHTIME

Maya has been selling handmade bracelets at her table. She started with 80 bracelets. She has 16 bracelets left.

Sorry, I didn't write down how many bracelets I have sold. Let's use subtraction to figure it out.

Robert and Maya work together. They write the total number of bracelets first. They add a minus sign, then the number of bracelets left.

$$80 - 16 = 64$$

Number of bracelets left

Total number of bracelets

Number of bracelets sold

Maya has sold 64 bracelets. Great job, Maya!

Ali's cupcake table has been very popular. He started off with 123 cupcakes. He has 38 cupcakes left. Ali scratches his head. He is having trouble subtracting large numbers. Luckily, Robert knows how to help.

I can't figure out how many cupcakes I have sold!

Robert draws a chart to help Ali subtract. Each column is a different place value: hundreds, tens, or ones. Each row has a different number. He writes the total number of cupcakes in the first row. He writes the number of cupcakes left in the second row.

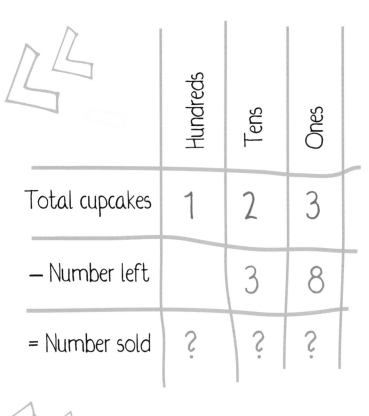

	Hundreds	Tens	Ones
Total cupcakes	1	2	3
− Number left		3	8
= Number sold	?	?	?

A ten is a **bundle** of ten ones. A hundred is a bundle of ten tens.

Robert shows Ali how to subtract each column.
First, they subtract the numbers in the ones column.
These numbers are three minus eight.

Ali is confused. It is impossible to take away a larger number from a smaller one! Robert explains. He can borrow one bundle of ten from the tens column. This makes 13 in the ones column. It leaves one in the tens column.

Hundreds	Tens	Ones
1	¹2̸	¹3
−	3	8
=		5

$$13 - 8 = 5$$

The last **digit** of the answer is 5.

ROBERT ROUNDS IT UP

Robert and Ali follow the same steps to subtract the numbers in the tens column. They borrow a bundle of one hundred from the hundreds column. This makes 11 in the tens column. It leaves zero in the hundreds column.

Hundreds	Tens	Ones
⁰1̸	¹¹2̸	¹3
−	3	8
= 8	8	5

11 − 3 = 8

There are no numbers left in the hundreds column. That means 85 is the answer.

$$123 - 38 = 85$$

Ali has sold 85 cupcakes.

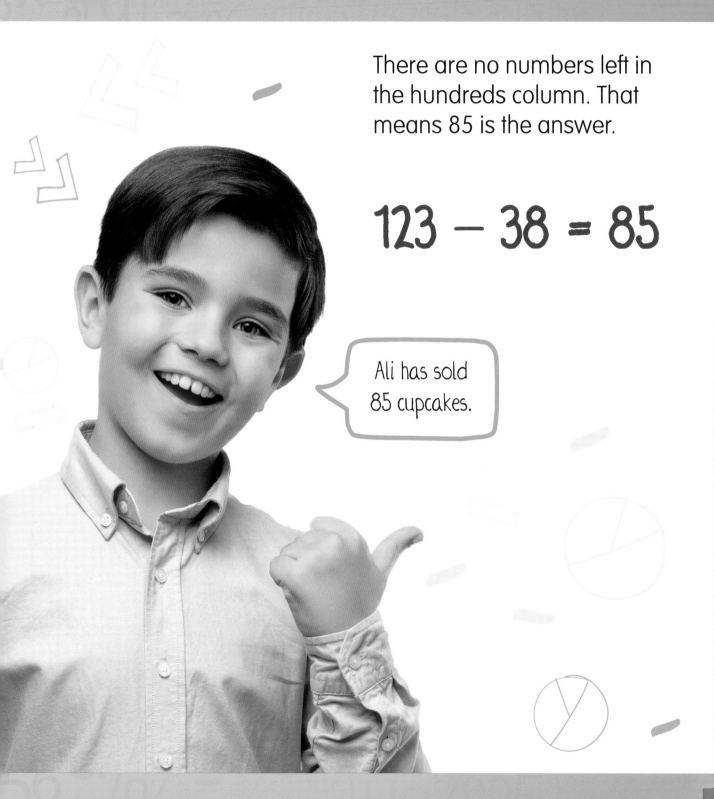

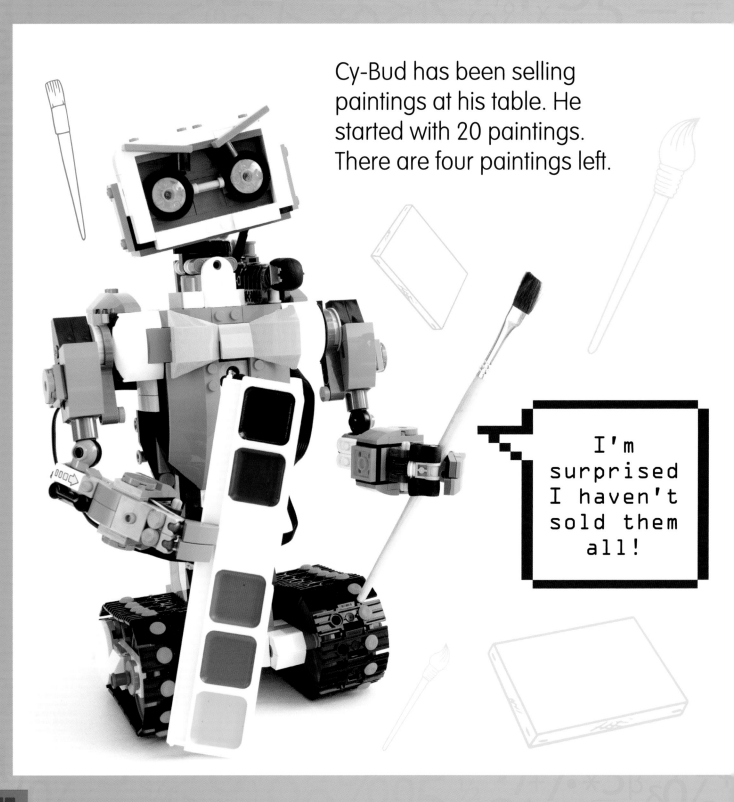

Cy-Bud has been selling paintings at his table. He started with 20 paintings. There are four paintings left.

I'm surprised I haven't sold them all!

We can use a number line to find out how many paintings Cy-Bud has sold. Number lines work well for subtracting smaller numbers. When we subtract, we count backward on a number line.

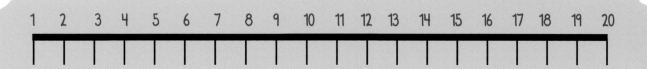

1 2 3 4 5 6 7 8 9 10 11 12 13 14 15 16 17 18 19 20

The number line makes counting forward and backward easier.

Robert starts at number 20. This is the number of paintings Cy-Bud had to start. Cy-bud has four paintings left. Robert uses his finger to count four numbers backward from 20. The number he lands on is the number of paintings sold.

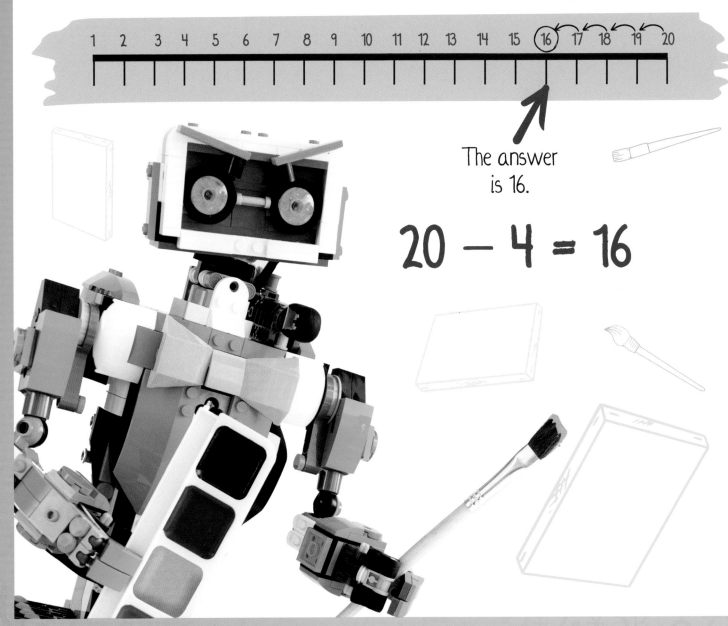

1 2 3 4 5 6 7 8 9 10 11 12 13 14 15 (16) 17 18 19 20

The answer is 16.

$$20 - 4 = 16$$

Robert takes the list of sold items to Professor Tangent.

Who	What	Number at Start		Number Left		Number Sold
Zoë	Lemonade	9	−	2	=	7
Maya	Bracelets	80	−	16	=	64
Ali	Cupcakes	123	−	38	=	85
Cy-Bud	Paintings	20	−	4	=	16

Excellent job today, everyone!

PROBLEM SOLVED

Ms. Wizz, the Principal of Math Academy, was so impressed by class 301's hard work. She decided to buy all of the items left!

I'll take them all!

The students are so excited. They have raised enough money to buy the super-calculator. Now, they just hope it gets along with Cy-Bud!

HOMEWORK

Can you use these charts to solve each problem?
Copy each chart into a notebook.

a)

Hundreds	Tens	Ones
1	9	3
−	8	7
Answer = ?	?	?

b)

Hundreds	Tens	Ones
3	7	5
− 1	5	4
Answer = ?	?	?

c)

Hundreds	Tens	Ones
2	3	5
− 1	2	1
Answer = ?	?	?

d)

Hundreds	Tens	Ones
8	5	3
− 3	9	6
Answer = ?	?	?

Answers: a)106, b)221, c)114, d)457

Can you use the number line to solve these problems?

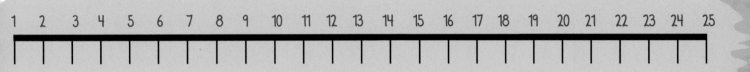

1 2 3 4 5 6 7 8 9 10 11 12 13 14 15 16 17 18 19 20 21 22 23 24 25

a) 23 − 9 = ?

e) 19 − 6 = ?

b) 20 − 10 = ?

f) 15 − 7 = ?

c) 24 − 21 = ?

g) 9 − 6 = ?

d) 13 − 4 = ?

Answers: a=14, b=10, c=3, d=9, e=13, f=8, g=3

GLOSSARY

CALCULATOR	A small device that is used for math
BUNDLE	Objects put together in a group, such as tens
CHARTS	Information in the form of a table
DIGIT	A written symbol for any of the numbers zero to nine
NUMBER LINES	A straight line with numbers evenly spaced along it
PLACE VALUE	The value of a digit based on its position in a number
SUBTRACTION	Taking one number away from another number
SYMBOL	A shape or mark that represents, or stands for, something else

INDEX